About This Guide

As a psychologist, the most common question I get asked is: "How do I find a therapist?" Most people are overwhelmed with options, and don't know where to start. Where do you look? What do all these qualifications mean? What are these different kinds of therapy? Does it matter what kind you choose?

I get it. Most therapists use lots of buzzwords like "dynamic" and "modalities", rather than speaking in terms that people understand. And what's the deal with all therapist websites looking like they're from 1999? Because the process can be so confusing and frustrating, many people give up before they find a good fit.

This is why I put together this guide. I wanted to provide at least a broad overview of what the heck is going on in the therapy world, and help you understand the parts that are most relevant to you. You'll find terms defined, credentials explained, and information provided so you can make a great therapist choice.

Armed with the information above, I hope you will feel more prepared to begin your therapy adventure.

Sincerely,

Dr. Janna R. Koretz

About The Author

Dr. Janna Koretz is a licensed psychologist and founder of Azimuth Psychological (*www.azimuthpsych.com*), which provides testing and therapy services in Boston, Cambridge, and Nantucket MA.

Dr. Koretz's specialty is in helping families understand the struggles of their adolescent children through testing data. Dr. Koretz is focused on finding ways to make therapy more accessible, useful, and relatable for a wide range of age groups.

Contents

Common Questions About Therapy

How do I know if I need to see a therapist, psychologist, or psychiatrist?

Therapist is a generic term that refers to anyone with some kind of training to help people with personal difficulties. A *psychologist* specifically refers to someone with a doctoral degree in psychology.

Although historically *psychiatrists* have provided therapy and medication, most modern psychiatrists only prescribe medication, and are not trained to provide therapy. So, if you're looking for a therapist, you would most likely be looking for a psychologist or other therapist (such as a social worker). If you or your therapist think medication may be helpful, you would also look for a psychiatrist.

These differences are outlined in more detail in the under the *Degrees and Licensing* section of this guide.

What is the difference between counseling, therapy, and psychotherapy?

Counseling tends to be a service provided by someone with a specific counseling degree. These programs tend to focus more on crisis intervention and specific problem resolution.

Psychotherapy (often shortened to just "therapy") tends to be a service provided by someone with an LMHC, social work, or psychology postgraduate degree (see the *Degrees and Licenses* section of this guide for more details).

Do I need to search on WebMD to see if I qualify for a diagnosis before I see a therapist?

A diagnosis is not required in order to attend therapy. Therapy can be helpful for many people, regardless of whether they meet criteria for a diagnosis or not. However, most insurance companies do require a diagnosis for reimbursement.

My therapist is dull and doesn't laugh at my cat memes. Should I keep seeing them for therapy?

A therapist's personality is a huge factor in the success of therapy. You'll want to find a therapist who is a good fit from a personality perspective. Because it could take a few sessions to really get a sense of your therapist's personality, it's a good idea to "try out" a therapist for a few visits before you decide if he or she is right for you.

My friend Jane is an awesome listener. Why am I not feeling better talking to her?

Jane is likely a good listener and great friend. But, she isn't trained to provide scientifically-validated coping strategies, problem solving techniques, and communication skills.

Therapists have many years of training and experience, and have gained some useful (and often counterintuitive) knowledge that not everybody has. This doesn't mean you shouldn't also keep talking to your friend Jane—just that a therapist will offer you something very different.

How does talking about something make it better?

Talking through your issues with a skilled therapist can help you understand why something is the way it is. It also helps with peace of mind, coping, problem solving, and preparedness.

The relationship you will develop with your therapist is also important. Having a trusting relationship with an outside party who has your best interests at heart promotes progress and well-being.

How do I know if I would benefit from therapy?

Therapy can be helpful in many different circumstances. A good rule of thumb is: if the issue you're facing interferes with your day-to-day ability to function at your best, then therapy is likely to be a useful part of the solution.

Does my therapist think I'm insane?

No. Your therapist's job is to help you with whatever you need, and he or she will be happy to have an opportunity to help you. Your therapist will look beyond the struggles you happen to be facing and see you as the whole person that you are.

I'm smart. Why can't I resolve things on my own?

Here's a secret: most therapists go to therapy. It even used to mandatory in some graduate psychology programs.

Why? Because it's important for therapists to understand themselves before they can effectively help others, and it's almost impossible to do that alone. Even when you are a professional therapist, the one person you can't help is yourself.

What is HIPAA?

HIPAA Stands for Health Insurance Portability and Accountability Act, which is a series of rules put into place in 2003 by the federal government to protect the privacy of healthcare consumers. It prohibits the distribution or discussion of your private health information without your written consent (with a few exceptions related to the safety of yourself and others).

So, how do I actually start looking for someone to see?

There are a few ways to start this process. Asking friends and family for personal recommendations is often a good option, although depending on your relationship with your friend or family member, you may not want to see the same person. But, you could still inquire with the recommended therapist for their own recommendations of their colleagues. Therapists are used to taking brief phone calls to help with the referral process.

You can also try searching on Psychology Today (*psychologytoday.com*), an expansive directory of therapists that can be filtered by location, insurance accepted, kind of therapy practiced, and many other details.

If the idea of combing through therapists online is daunting, There is a service called Sophia (*trysophia.com*) that can help. Sophia is a therapist matching  service that helps you find a therapist that's right for you. After filling out a brief survey about what you're looking for, Sophia's system matches you to a short list of local therapists that are likely to be a good fit.

Can I schedule an appointment for someone else?

Typically if the person seeking therapy is over 18, they make the appointment themselves to maintain confidentiality.

Therapy Myths & Misconceptions

I'll have to lie on a couch, and I'm not really into that

While lying on a couch and free-associating was part of the drill a long time ago, it's now only required when working with a therapist using a psychoanalytic approach (see the *Approaches and Techniques* section of this guide for more details).

For the most part, you'll be sitting on a chair or couch facing the therapist. But, if you're worried about it, you can always ask when inquiring about a session. Therapists answer this question often, so no need to feel shy!

The therapist will say nothing and give me no direction

Some therapists are more directive or participatory, and some are less so. The therapist's technique depends on their personality as well as their training. Most modern clinicians fall somewhere in between.

If this is a concern for you, be sure to ask; most therapists don't write about their participation style on their website or clinical profiles, so it will be up to you to bring it up.

My therapist will do inappropriate things that make me uncomfortable, like in the Sopranos

Psychologists and most other therapists are required to adhere to an ethics code in order to maintain their license. They are also required to adhere to all HIPAA regulations. The provisions of both the ethics code and HIPAA are designed to protect your rights and your well-being as a client.

For details on HIPAA, visit: *www.hhs.gov/hipaa*

For details on the American Psychological Association (APA) Ethics code, visit: *www.apa.org/ethics/code/*

This therapist doesn't have a website, or their site looks like it's from the 90's. They must not be legit

Many therapists do not place high value on technology or websites. This may be due to lack of interest, belief that analog is more appropriate, or simply a lack of time. As a result, many well-qualified therapists do not have a good online presence or technological capabilities in their office (e.g., many of them do not accept credit cards). So, lack of a good website shouldn't necessarily be a red flag.

If a therapist is recommended to you by someone you trust, or looks interesting to you based on the information you can find about them online, it's always best to follow up to gain more information. It may end up being a great fit!

If I go to therapy, I am committing to going for the long term

Therapy can be any length of time. It really depends on what you're working on. Some people also find that, even when they've reached their goals, they like having an independent expert to talk with about their life, and for that reason they continue to go.

Degrees and Licenses

There are a number of different degrees and licenses that your therapist might have. Here is a list of the most common therapy-related degrees and what they mean.

But first, a word about licenses...

Being licensed is important, because it means the clinician you're seeing has participated in an approved educational program and has passed a board examination. This ensures that the clinician has all the required education and clinical experience that the state and national boards have determined are necessary in order to help others. If you see someone who is not licensed, you will just have to take their word for it that their training and experience is satisfactory—something I don't recommend!

Doctoral-Level

If someone has a Ph.D. or a Psy.D. after their name, that indicates that they have completed a doctoral-level program in psychology. Clinicians with these degrees are are the only people who can legally call themselves "psychologists".

One of these degrees isn't "better" or more difficult than the other; both programs focus on human psychology and issues such as depression and anxiety. The main distinction is that, in general, Psy.D. psychologists focus more on clinical work during their doctorate, while Ph.D. psychologists focus more on research.

Master's-Level

Master's-level degrees include social work degrees such as Licensed Independent Clinical Social Worker (LICSW), Licensed Social Worker (LSW), and Licensed Clinical Social Worker (LCSW). These are individuals who have completed their master's degree in social work. They are often referred to as "therapists" or "clinicians", but cannot legally use the term "psychologist".

Traditionally, social work degrees focused more on social systems, case management, and environmental factors. Today, however, many social work training programs incorporate psychology and clinical work as well.

Other masters-level degrees can include Licensed Mental Health Counselor (LMHC) and Licensed Marriage and Family Therapist (MFT). An MFT degree focuses specifically on couples and family therapy.

Other Degrees

As you look for a therapist, you may also encounter people with Psychiatrist (MD) and Psychiatric Mental Health Nurse Practitioner (PMHNP) degrees. These professionals usually focus on prescribing medication, but some will also do therapy with their clients.

If medication is helpful for you, it is not uncommon to work with a therapist and a psychiatrist at the same time. If you don't have a psychiatrist but need one, your therapist will often be able to provide some recommendations.

Therapy Approaches
& Techniques

Many therapists' websites give you the technical name for their approach, but don't include an explanation of what that means for you. Below are the details of some popular approaches to therapy.

Cognitive Behavioral Therapy (CBT)

This is a popular type of therapy that highlights how our thoughts impact our emotions and actions, even when we don't realize it. A main focus of CBT is building skills to consciously identify and rearrange thinking patterns that are unhelpful or inaccurate.

Dialectical Behavioral Therapy (DBT)

DBT is popular for clinicians helping individuals suffering from Borderline Personality Disorder (BPD), focusing on topics such as mindfulness and interpersonal skills.

"True" DBT is done in a group format, with weekly meetings with a skills coach who is on call 24/7. However, many clinicians incorporate some aspects of DBT into their work on a less formal basis.

Acceptance and Commitment Therapy (ACT)

ACT includes some CBT principles, but also incorporates aspects of acceptance and mindfulness. Eliminating negative feelings is not the goal; instead to goal is to identify and accept them. The goal is to help you move forward with an ability to observe yourself and to choose to act differently in the moment.

Psychoanalysis and Psychodynamic Therapy

Psychoanalytic theory was developed by Sigmund Freud. In this theory, there are three parts of the brain (the Id, the Ego, and the Superego) that combine to cause you to behave in certain ways. There is also the concept of "defense mechanisms" that are used unconsciously to keep negative thoughts at bay.

In psychoanalysis, clients often lay on the couch and free-associate. The focus is on the internal world of the client.

Psychodynamic theory is derived from Freud's original psychoanalytic theory, with a specific focus on the therapist-client relationship.

Mindfulness-Based Therapy

Mindfulness means keeping focus in the present, instead of focusing on the past or future. Mindfulness exercises are meant to train the brain to simply notice thoughts that come into your mind, let them go, and focus on the here and now. Mindfulness has been incorporated into many different therapy approaches.

What about text-based and phone therapy?

There are many services and clinicians that provide support via text or video chat. Although those tools can be helpful, many kinds of therapy are based on being present with someone in the same room.

The nuances of body language and emotional moments are difficult to convey over the phone. For this reason, some therapists won't provide remote therapy, or will only participate in remote sessions once they have become familiar with you through in-person sessions.

Starting Therapy

Typically, the process to make an appointment is:

1. Call or email the therapist to make your initial appointment (or to find out more information before making your appointment).

2. Once the appointment is made, you will usually need to complete some forms including your personal and contact information. These forms will usually also inform you about your privacy rights and the policies of the office. Forms can be sent to you ahead of time, but will also generally be available for you to fill out at the first appointment.

3. Enjoy your first appointment! Therapy can feel weird at first, so trying out your therapist for three or four sessions is usually recommended so you can get a good sense of how you might work together.

Questions to ask when making a therapy appointment

Here are some questions you may want to ask of a prospective therapist. This focuses on personality and approach; for financial and insurance questions, go to the *Using Insurance* section of this guide.

- What approach do you use?

- What kinds of clients do you have?

- Do you have a specialty?

- What make you unique?

- Who is your ideal client?

- What type of client would *not* be a good fit for you?

Using Insurance

Health insurance is difficult to understand and ever-changing. Here are some answers to the most frequently asked questions, as well as a comprehensive list of what to ask your insurance company when you call them to inquire about your benefits.

Remember, insurance plans are very different from one another, and change often. Because of this, it is always best to call your insurance company directly.

How much am I going to have to pay?

This depends on whether your therapist is "in network" or "out of network". If you are "in network" and have a deductible, you will need to pay the session fee to your therapist until your deductible is satisfied. If you are "in network" and don't have a deductible (or your deductible has already been satisfied), you will just pay your co-pay.

If you are "out of network", you will pay the full fee to your therapist at the time of your appointment. Your therapist will then provide an invoice that you can submit to your insurance company for reimbursement.

I have insurance, so why am I being charged?

If you get a bill from your therapist even though you thought you were covered by your insurance, there are a couple reasons this might have happened.

1. You may have a deductible that needs to be satisfied before your benefits kick in. In this instance, if your therapist charged you, it is because your insurance company told them that you are responsible for payment until your deductible is satisfied.

2. You may have a copay that is different than what you expected, and the bill represents the difference between what you have already paid and what you still owe.

What happens if it turns out insurance doesn't cover my appointments?

If insurance does not cover your sessions, you are responsible for the full cost. This is why, if you intend to use your insurance to help pay for therapy, it is very important to first call your insurance company to verify your benefits.

What questions should I ask my insurance company before scheduling an appointment?

When you call your insurance company, you'll want to ask them a few questions to understand your benefits more clearly. Before you call, look up your desired therapist's NPI number at *npiregistry.cms.hhs.gov* so you can give it to your insurance company.

1. Is the therapist I want to see considered "in network"?

2. *(If your desired therapist is not "in network")* Do I have out-of-network benefits?

3. Do I have a deductible? If so, how much is it, and how much has been satisfied to date? What is my copay?

4. *(If you do not have out-of-network benefits)* Do I have a separate deductible for out-of-network expenses, and how much will I be reimbursed? *(Make sure to ask for a specific number, not just a percentage)*

There's an app for that!

Better is an app that helps you get reimbursed by your health insurance for visiting  an out-of-network therapist. Here's how it works:

1. Visit *getbetter.co* to sign up and download the iPhone app or Android-compatible web app

2. Take a photo of the bill inside the app, or email *claims@getbetter.co* with your "super bill" attached

3. They work with your insurance to get you paid, and take a small fee out of your reimbursement check as payment